迷航烏托邦

科技世界讓人生迷路，但你依舊還可以很幸福

Lost In Utopias

文/葉向林　圖/披薩先生

作者簡介

葉向林 Noah

在區塊鏈新創設定現實又充滿想像力的未來競爭及協作策略。第一位進入美國帕森設計學院全球高管碩士就讀的台灣人,同時也是 NFL 超級盃主播與美式足球運動員。

插畫者簡介

披薩先生 PIZZA!

插畫家 / 大學講師 / 模型店老闆 / 開小 MARCH 的人。

Glen Weyl │ 激進市場作者

I was excited to read this inviting and vivid
representation of the diversity of possible
technological futures made accessible to young children.
I hope my daughters will gain wisdom and
hope from reading this beautiful little book.

王志仁 │ 數位時代總編輯

有點像區塊鏈版的《小王子》，
輕巧易讀但耐人尋味。

矽谷阿雅｜矽谷人工智慧新創執行長

雖然我住在科技第一線的矽谷，

但 Noah 是我見過走在最世界最前衛、

最有思考力的創新人了，

但另一方面，Noah 又是一位真誠、充滿智慧、

有些「宅」的知識豐富好奇寶寶。

這不僅是一本童書，也是一本適合大人看的勵志書，

就像經典名著《小王子》一樣，

它充滿了智慧和省思，

你在找人生的烏托邦嗎？

你覺得自己不完美嗎？

你希望你的孩子快樂且知足嗎？

這是一本必讀的好書！

邵懿文│電通行銷傳播集團數位長

這本童書讀來新奇而有趣。

新奇之處在於，

這應該是第一本給 Z 世代和他的孩子共享的科技童書吧；

有趣之處在於，小狐狸的旅程超級精彩生動，

道出 web3 世界的思路又有哲學意味，

令人緊緊跟隨。

侯宜秀│律師／零時政府揪松團輪值主席

小狐狸彷彿從小王子的身邊走來，

告訴我們那些從 web0 到 web3 恆長時間中反復傳誦的故事，

關於建立、連結與烏托邦的追尋。

胡晉華｜Twitch 台港內容總監

哈囉，你迷路了嗎？

讀著一本童書，想著是大人的自己，

上一次無憂無慮的捧心大笑是什麼時候呢？

長大以後的快樂，永遠好像缺了一個角。

在《迷航烏托邦》裡，我們跟著小狐狸，

探訪了每一個嚮往中的美好，

誠心推薦十歲到一百歲的孩子，

可以在尋找快樂的過程中，喚醒自己的色彩。

黃彥霖｜FAB DAO 創辦人

葉向林透過小狐狸的探索旅程，

折射其個人於科技業界二十餘年的省思，

並以童話故事向技術文明的終點提問，人類最終將走向何方。

當虛擬情感、可交換財貨、知識語意網絡、

注意力經濟獲得無限滿足，那是幸福的終點嗎？

《迷航烏托邦》同時也成為作者個人下一段旅程的指引，

希望有機會也邀您同行。

鄒德平｜知名專業口譯

眞心推薦的一本好書！
雖然作者當初跟我說這是一本「童書」，
但個人認爲，這本書之老少咸宜，
從還在學習識字閱讀的小學生，到學過文本解讀的文學人，
乃至於任何對科技發展充滿興趣與想像的每一個人，
相信讀完這本書之後都能夠激發出不同的想法、有所收穫！

寶博士｜電通集團 Web3 成長顧問

「沒有去中心」因爲當有人對你說「該要去中心」他就成了中心；
「沒有哪裡是烏托邦」因爲哪裡說是，哪裡也許就不再是了。
佛曰：不可說。
經文說：色卽是空，空卽是色。
小狐狸說：烏托邦不在哪裡，也都在哪裡。

Melissa Rancourt ｜帕森斯全球高管碩士學院總監

Lost Utopias is a beautiful and soulful illustration of what can be created from a deep-rooted need to find a solution to a what we refer to as a 'wicked problem'. Hsiang-Lin Yeh, the author, is one of the members of a global executive Master's degree experience in Strategic Design for Global Leadership at Parsons School of Design in New York, Paris and Shanghai. Through his studies in this program, Hsiang-Lin contemplated, just as Lost Utopias' Little Fox, the juxtapositions that push and pull us, as a society, and that create both solutions and sometimes, often, more problems. In the most empathetic and caring way, which is at the heart of the Strategic Design process, Hsiang-Lin searched for ways to help us with wicked quandaries such as happiness and capitalism, data and altruism,friendships and technology.

And through his search, the Little Fox emerged.

Read Lost Utopias and you may see your own quest through a different lens.

Melissa Rancourt, Senior Director for the executive program, MS in Strategic Design for Global Leadership at Parsons School of Design at The New School

葉文心 ｜柏克萊加州大學資深講座教授

　　每個人的經歷都可以成爲書。然而並不是每個人都能寫成書。向林跨出了這一步，把近二十年來的摸索與追尋表述成爲《迷航烏托邦》。這個書寫，提煉了他曾經有過的雜陳五味，凝聚了他靜下心來的反思。這是十分值得欣喜的。這本書的目的，不是自傳，也不是報導。但是因爲向林寫作的誘因與素材，得自他現實生活中眞切的情境，所以我們大可以把這部作品看成二十一世紀新一代人所記錄下來的心路歷程與時代側影。

　　向林是一個什麼樣的人？他跟這個新的大時代是如何銜接的呢？向林在大學以及研究所讀的是經濟與傳媒行銷。學成之後在職場上的第一個工作是雅虎。他正逢靑壯，這就注定了他在工作領域中見證了二十一世紀傳媒與科技的接軌，認識到大數據程式如何對傳統行銷策略產生革命性的衝擊。在他的工作領域中，商機與訊息正透過龐大的機械複製能量，以排山倒海的勢頭日益強大地滲透進大眾的日常生活中。在他所研讀的專業書籍文章裡，他讀到新知識相應於新發展，如何跨出傳統商學院、傳媒學科的經典內涵，在批判意識跟實踐邏輯之間重複擺盪，如何層出不窮地一再由立而破，由破而又立。這是個令人眼花撩亂的工作與讀書環境。而在其間，資本主義的世界舞台上同時又出現了一些橫空獨步的新型菁英人物。這些菁英亮麗悅目，左右了時尚話語，透過科技的包裝與仲介，有人許諾無遠弗屆、無時不在的溫情，有人導引如何開發新的滾滾財源，有人提供無邊無盡的信息資訊。每個全球插旗的大業都有一片跨聯多國的版圖，都有一套免費服務人生、增添快樂、點石成金、排難解憂的敘述。然而這些大業在創造財富、包裝知識與網絡友誼的同時，不但重新分配了這些資源，同時也創造了新的不公、不均、失真、與失落。

　　向林在這個岩漿噴發的新世界中是一個走出自然村，搭橋問路、尋仙訪道的年輕小人物。他在《迷航烏托邦》之中把自己寫成一隻別人看不見的透明小狐狸，內心充滿了焦慮與孤寂。他的焦慮推動了一次又一次的追尋，他在嘗試了種種探索之後，在點點滴滴的過程中一方面認識了自己，一方面認識到大世界的形貌與邏輯。《迷航烏托邦》是這個歷程的沉澱與收穫。這本書結合了寓言與科幻的成分，以清晰明快的筆法，以交響樂樂章式的結構，把小狐狸在科技化新世界中的摸索，繪寫成為多元多樣的景觀。《迷航烏托邦》是為小狐狸以及小小狐狸們寫的。題目雖然叫作「迷航」，但是卻是解迷、導航的嘗試，就跟其他大海孤舟或大漠迷途的作品一般。這是一本很值得一讀的小書。今天科技重構了時空，虛擬跟實體的身分場景交錯共存，二十一世紀的世界是個多維度、失重、去中心的世界，也是系統性體系操作無所不到的世界。我希望大家在讀完這本書之後，也跟向林一般，提起筆來，啟航烏托邦，為自己尋找座標，同時也摸索這個新時代。

For my parents & GEMSV
In memory of my beloved grandma

目 錄

我想我們仍是為了社會健全與個人快樂在努力著，

但科技並不總是扮演幫忙的角色。

故事裡的烏托邦們都影射著某類型的科技帝國，

在你讀這本書的時候不妨把自己放到小狐狸的身體裡，

想想與這些科技承諾互動的自己，

是否真的找到了快樂，是否真的找到了價值。

狐狸村

Village Of The Foxes

狐狸村是個和平的地方，狐狸們每天不是陶醉地跳舞，就是歡笑著聊天，宇宙裡大概沒幾個這樣的地方。

　　但即使是狐狸村也有例外，小狐狸雖然心裡也天天想著跳舞聊天，但總是無法陶醉歡笑。他生來就沒有顏色，總是跟背景融爲一體，即使積極博取村民注意，對方的注意力幾乎總在瞬間就轉移到別人身上。不管他多麼想要交到朋友，從來都是以失敗收場。

　　狐狸村雖然三天兩頭就找事來慶祝，但沒有什麼比狐火節更盛大的活動了。沒有顏色的小狐狸早就做好了準備，他一定要在今晚陶醉歡笑，他一定要在今晚交到朋友。

　　In a metaverse far, far away, there lay a peaceful village inhabited by foxes.

　　One of the villagers was unlike any other. Despite trying hard to get noticed, to be seen, to make friends, he was never successful. That villager was a little fox born without color.

　　The village's harvest festival had arrived. That night, he was eager to participate in the celebrations, longing to make some friends.

All the foxes there held paws and formed a circle, dancing and singing around the fire.

The little fox jumped around the circle hoping to find an empty spot. There was none. He grew anxious and sped up his step.

He couldn't tell if it was a piece of wood or someone's foot that he stepped on. Next thing he knew, his face was covered in dirt.

The other foxes noticed him and started laughing. In his eyes though, they seemed happy. Something amazing happened, the little fox's face and body started to show colors that he had never seen before. He was filled with excitement.

Yet as the foxes got back to dancing, the colors slowly faded.

"I need to make others happy," the little fox concluded.

村子中央的空地燃燒著熊熊營火，燒到快跟房子一樣高了。星空下的狐狸們手牽手、掌對掌，愉快地與彼此連結著。他們的歌聲穿透了村子周圍的黑暗，讓遠方的陌生人也可以感受到快樂的氛圍。

　　小狐狸周圍瀰漫的快樂似乎與他毫無關係。他焦慮得像裝了噴射引擎的月球一樣繞著大圓圈公轉，他得盡快找到個空位加入。但不管他步伐再大、呼吸再急，空位就是不出現。也許是小狐狸的幻覺，他每跑一圈都覺得村民間的距離好像更小了。

　　不知道是絆到了樹枝還是某人的腳，小狐狸意識過來的時候已經滿臉塵土，四肢僵直的飛撲在地。

　　忍著疼痛起身的他聽到周圍的笑聲，起初也不以為意，狐狸村哪天沒有笑聲，但他卻發現這些笑聲越來越近，原來村民們正指著他笑。不經世事的小狐狸只覺得村民看起來似乎很快樂，甚至還有人抱著肚子倒在地上。不一會兒神奇的事發生了，小狐狸的身上開始出現從未有過的顏色。

　　他又驚又喜，等回過神來想跟村民們說話時，村民們早就回到營火旁的大圓圈裡了，連笑倒在地的那位都恢復了冷靜，小狐狸低頭看看自己的身體，顏色消失了。

　　「我得讓大家快樂。」小狐狸默默地下了這個結論。

A wandering witch at the festival overheard and said to him, "Why don't you visit the utopias? You might learn a thing or two about making others happy."

The witch continued, "Outside of this small village, there are many utopias

「你怎麼不試著去拜訪那些烏托邦呢？」巫女毫無聲息的出現在小狐狸身後，他的毛髮像卡通般因驚嚇而豎立，連轉身都轉得相當僵硬。巫女的身材修長，看起來很有智慧，小狐狸身心都得抬得高高的才能好好跟她說話。雖然心裡有點詫異巫女怎麼會突然出現在他身旁，但他知道問了也沒用，巫女不就是這樣來去無蹤的嗎？

　　「在你的小村子外，有很多追求快樂的烏托邦。每個烏托邦都有個國王，他們對自己的人民也都承諾了更快樂的明天，他們是這些烏托邦的英雄。」巫女跟著說。「去那些烏托邦旅行也許能幫你找到快樂的祕密。」

　　抬著頭的小狐狸脖子雖然有點痠，但眼裡的光芒卻從來沒有那麼閃耀過。

created by great kings.

　　Every great king promises a better tomorrow. They are heroes to the citizens of the utopias."

　　The little fox's eyes had never shone so brightly.

"Before you travel," The witch added,
"you must bring a hammer." She then pulled some tools from a dusty old bag. "You must build your way forward."

The little fox saw three hammers in front of him, one small, one big, and one in between.

"They all weigh the same," the witch said. "Choose one for your journey."

The little fox picked the biggest hammer, hoping to set out on the greatest adventure.

All of a sudden, the sky shot forth a silver flash, dazzling the little fox and the witch. The little fox squinted its eyes hard to see the mysterious burst better, but it vanished into the witch's bag all too soon.

"Good luck learning to make others happy," said the witch before bidding him farewell.

"I will." The little fox took the first step of his journey convinced that he'd at last find his color.

「在你出發以前，」巫女似乎認定小狐狸一定會踏上自己建議的旅程。

　　「你得選擇一隻槌子。」巫女將身後的烏黑布袋放到地上，大量灰塵從表面掉落，好像從沒被清理過似的，跟巫女本身形成強烈對比。沒意外的話地上的螞蟻窩已經像龐貝城般被滅村了。

　　「你得打造你自己的路。」

　　「這些槌子的重量都是一樣的，」巫女接著說「爲你的旅程選擇一隻吧。」

　　小狐狸看著大小不同的三隻槌子，決定爲他最偉大的旅程選擇最大的槌子。

　　小狐狸與巫女的正上方突然擦出了些銀色閃光，小狐狸還沒細看那銀色閃光就已經被巫女收進了背包裡。「一路順風。」巫女頭也不回的轉身走了，只留下了一句「希望你能找到快樂的祕密。」。

　　「我會的。」小狐狸很堅決，他相信總有一天他會找到自己的顏色。

烏托邦 I

挚友工廠
Best Friend Factory

如果瞇起眼睛仔細看的話，似乎真的可以朦朧看到狐狸村外城鎮的輪廓，但別說是小狐狸了，村裡從來沒有任何人有去過這麼遠的地方。

　　「我得打造我自己的路。」小狐狸重複著巫女的話。

　　他將大槌子高高舉起，興奮的想像著他即將搭建的完美大橋。

The little fox could catch a glimpse of the closest utopia from his village, but no fox had ever traveled that far before.

"I'll build my way forward."

The little fox wielded his hammer and started to build the most perfect bridge he could conceive.

The mighty hammer chipped away bit by bit with every strike at a rock, yet this did not deter the little fox. The utopia awaited.

The finished bridge was far from perfect, but it could do. Not much of the hammer remained, yet all that mattered to the little fox was reaching the utopia.

A gate appeared at the end of the bridge. The inscription above the gate read "Never Alone".

The little fox spotted a long line of citizens in front of a factory, waiting with uncontained anticipation. This awoke his curiosity.

大槌子的密度不高，從空洞的敲擊聲就可以聽得出來。而麻煩的不是聲音，槌子的表面每次與石頭撞擊後就會立刻缺角，槌子越敲越小，形狀也越發怪異。但這些對小狐狸來說都不重要，除了缺乏回饋感的敲擊偶爾讓他眉頭微皺之外，他眼裡現在只有等著他的快樂烏托邦。

　　橋是建完了，但它一點都不完美，歪掉的拱心石明顯只是勉強支撐著橋的結構。橋的地面凹凸不平，幸好小狐狸沒有踩到那些較深的坑洞，不然他大概得試著用槌子把腳給敲出來。

　　雖然橋看起來不太完美，但至少還算完整，相反的風光一時的大槌子早已面目全非，實在看不出它曾有任何威猛的過去。小狐狸不在意，用輕快的腳步快速到達彼岸，橋的終點處有扇木頭建成的大門，這扇門感覺挺親切的，不像是會拒人於外的樣子。小狐狸揉揉眼睛看了門頂的刻字，上面寫著「永不孤單」。

走進大門後小狐狸立刻注意到街道上那條長長的隊伍，他轉了好幾個街角才見到隊伍的終點。終點處等著他的是一棟大型的木製建築，三根煙囪不斷排放著笑臉形狀的煙霧，不知道是座什麼樣的工廠。排隊的人們看起來相當期待，一直不斷向前打聽隊伍前進的進度。這個景象激起了小狐狸的好奇心。

　　「你們排隊在等什麼呢？」小狐狸好奇的問。

　　「我們在等最新的摯友。」居民用熱心的口氣回答。

　　「最新的摯友是什麼意思？」好奇瞬間變成了疑惑。

　　「我們已經想了好幾週怎麼設計我們的好朋友，只要你對國王提出要求，他都能做到。國王還說他會用最好的木材來打造摯友。不像那些冰冷的金屬，木材更能帶出摯友溫馨人性的一面。」小狐狸被居民的興奮感染，不自覺得也踏入了隊伍中。

"What are you all lining up for?" the little fox asked.

"Our new best friends," a citizen of the utopia replied.

"What do you mean by new best friends?" A look of puzzlement crossed the little fox's face.

"We've been thinking for weeks what our best friends should look like. The king promised he'd make our best friends out of the best quality wood in the forest. Not cold lifeless metal, but warm smooth wood!"

The little fox felt intrigued and immediately joined the queue of citizens.

After hours of waiting, it was finally his turn.

"Please describe the best friend of your dreams," the friendship king responsible for building the factory said in a friendly tone.

"My best friend should be loyal and follow me everywhere."

The king nodded and got down to work. He picked up a piece of light-hearted pine wood. It giggled at every chisel. The king made this best friend about the same height and weight as the little fox.

"Here you are, your new best friend!"

隊伍的確很長，但國王的效率似乎比開始時更高，隊伍縮短的速度讓小狐狸想多觀賞一下這個溫馨的木造城鎮都不行，不知不覺他已經站在國王面前了。

　　「你看起來不像我們烏托邦裡的居民。」雖然嘴上這麼說，國王的手卻沒有停下來。

　　「我是友好國王，請你形容一下夢想中的摯友模樣。」雖然手上忙碌不斷，但友好的國王仍保持友善的詢問口氣。當然為了基本禮貌，他的眼神也從來沒從小狐狸身上移開過。

　　「我想要一個永遠忠心而且支持我的朋友。」

　　友好國王笑著點了點頭，繼續加快他的工作速度。他拿起了一塊成色均勻而且質地滑順的松木，在佈滿木屑的桌上開始輕輕敲打。小狐狸發誓國王一開始輕敲的那幾下松木還發出了笑聲，像在搔癢一樣。

　　不一會兒小狐狸的新摯友就完成了。像小狐狸一樣它有著天真的眼神，就這麼直瞪瞪的看著小狐狸，不一樣的是摯友留了一抹似乎永遠擦不掉的微笑。

　　「好了，你的全新摯友。」

新摯友就像友好國王承諾的一樣忠心。小狐狸昨天講的三個笑話總計換得了摯友四次大笑與兩滴因笑過頭而擠出的眼淚。若是小狐狸想認真討論些什麼，新摯友一定正襟危坐，而且眼神充滿期待。不管小狐狸走到哪，摯友都像影子般隨形，隨時準備好各種忠心表演。

　　也不清楚時間過了多久，小狐狸與摯友從沒離開彼此的視線範圍，對彼此的依賴也逐漸加深。他們一直互相支持，即使是偷竊友好國王的木材做蹺蹺板，或是拿著彈弓追逐驚嚇四散的流浪貓，他們的忠誠都不曾改變，摯友就算沒笑出聲，臉上也永遠掛著微笑。

The little fox's new wooden friend was loyal as promised and supportive too. It laughed at every single joke the little fox told and responded with a big smile to whatever he said. No matter where the little fox went, his best friend was always by his side, ready to smile broadly and burst into laughter whenever the little fox needed encouragement.

Days, weeks, months went by. The little fox spent every moment with his new best friend and with nobody else. Even when the little fox stole a piece of wood from the factory just to build a seesaw or when he made fun of a blind street cat, his best friend would do nothing but giggle and grin.

One morning, the friendship king said he had to go away for a day, during which time the magic would vanish temporarily.

The little fox let his wooden friend rest at home and walked on the street alone for the first time in a long while.

這天天才剛亮，小狐狸就聽到友好國王對烏托邦的全民廣播。雖然友好國王的聲音十分慈祥，但睡夢中的小狐狸還是覺得刺耳。跟每天早上一樣，小狐狸第一件事就是轉頭望向跪坐在床邊的摯友，他還是保持著一貫的笑容，小狐狸也因此感到安心。

　　小狐狸張開耳朵，決定多少聽聽友好國王說了些什麼。「……將離開三天去參與烏托邦的領袖會議，屆時摯友魔法會暫時失去效力，各位居民請……」，小狐狸一轉頭就發現摯友的眼睛在緩緩閉上，跪坐的雙腿似乎也失去了支撐的氣力，身體就這樣向側邊倒下，直接靠著床沿，遠看就像是睡著了的小狐狸一樣。

　　小狐狸見摯友睡得熟，便不打算移動它。家裡的玩伴既然睡著了，不如就自己出去走走吧。小狐狸已經忘了上次一個人上街是什麼感覺了，心裡甚至還有點緊張。

因爲摯友沉睡而上街走動的居民們意外的多，有人穿著誇大高調，有人則高聲歌唱，他們不時會看向圍觀的群衆（如果有人圍觀的話），好像在等著他們給予讚賞與掌聲似的。

　　「好醜的褲子。」路過小狐狸身邊的居民低聲地說。

　　小狐狸有點詫異，他的確從村裡出來後就沒特別換過褲子，但也從來沒人跟他說過自己的褲子有問題，越想越惱怒。

　　「你長得也不怎麼好看。」小狐狸很久沒見過這麼多皺褶的眉頭了，眉頭下方的那張嘴接著吐出的話也不怎麼好聽。小狐狸越聽越氣，不斷講出腦裡蹦出的氣話，但對方一抓住小狐狸衣領，他就再也想不起接下來的事了。

　　"What an ugly pair of trousers," he said about a citizen who walked past him. "What a pathetic nobody," the citizen replied in an offended voice. Both continued to speak minds and eventually got into a fight. So did everyone else. The utopia descended into chaos.

再睜開眼睛時小狐狸正躺在街道正中央，天雖然已經黑了，但小狐狸附近仍然不斷出現吵架與木頭的蹦碎聲，「摯友無法創造烏托邦，」小狐狸默默地想著「不是所有人在這都是開心的。」瘀青的眼眶也開始紅了起來。

小狐狸走回自己的住處，拿起了背包與槌子，瞄了一眼仍然躺在床邊的摯友。閉著眼的摯友臉上還掛著微笑。為了讓自己記住這次的教訓，小狐狸將摯友的微笑拆了下來，放進自己的背包中。

沒有了笑容的摯友看起來像是會長眠百年似的，動也不動。小狐狸哀傷的看了摯友最後一眼，離開了他的第一個烏托邦。

"Best friends aren't enough to make utopias," the little fox thought to himself. "Not everyone is happy here."

He headed back to his dwelling and picked up his hammer. He gazed at his wooden friend one last time. Desirous of a reminder, he grabbed its wooden smile and put it in his bag.

Now smileless, it seemed as if his best friend would just sit there, dormant for hundreds of years.

Disappointed, the little fox walked away from his first utopia.

受到雪莉、特克爾教授的研究啟發，
對社群網站、人工智慧、數位友誼的反思。
只有面對與眞人來往的酸甜苦辣，才有眞正的情誼。

Inspired by Professor Sherry Turkle,
Reflections on social media, AI, and digital friendships
Only by facing the ups and downs of real-life interactions
can there be true friendship.

烏托邦 II

金鵝幣
Token Goose

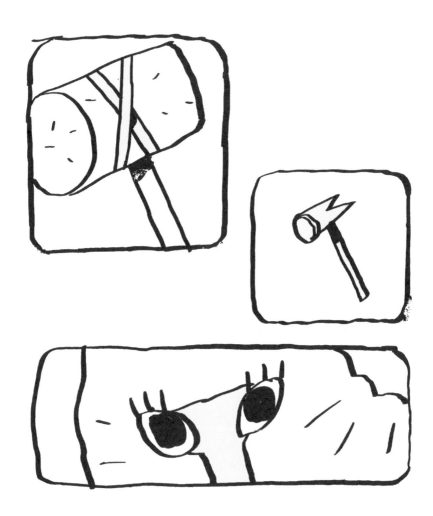

小狐狸看了看手上的槌子（或是那奇形怪狀的木塊），知道槌子大概已經耗盡了生命，沒有辦法再造另一座橋了，如果要繼續他的烏托邦旅程，他得回頭去找巫女才行。

　　巫女並不像想像的那樣來去無蹤，甚至還沒走到村裡就找到了。她微笑的坐在橋上望著遠遠走來的他，如果不說清楚，小狐狸甚至會覺得巫女有想誇獎他的意思。但仔細想了想，小狐狸打造的橋破破爛爛，巫女送他的槌子也毀了，更別說找到快樂了，實在是沒有什麼值得鼓勵的地方。

　　After taking another look at what was left of his hammer, the little fox realized he wouldn't be able to build another bridge with it. He had to see the witch again.

「這些槌子的重量都是一樣的，」巫女的說詞還是那樣，這次指著剩下的兩個槌子「為你的旅程選擇一隻吧。」。

巫女看起來一樣充滿智慧，她的微笑就像是在告訴小狐狸必須做自己的選擇，不能依靠別人。小狐狸撅著嘴想了想自己學到的教訓，用拇指和食指夾起了那隻較小的槌子。抬起頭巫女還是親切地看著他，但他實在等不及彌補自己的錯誤，決定快速回到建橋的工作上。

一如想像的小槌子並沒有任何碎裂，甚至還扎實得很，每一下敲擊都發出響亮的鏗鏘聲。經過一陣打擊後，小狐狸用迷你的槌子建了一座迷你的橋。

這座小橋小到小狐狸只能單腳踏上，上橋就像上鋼索一樣吃力，還得隨時保持平衡。最糟糕的是這個橋不但窄，同時也短得很，下一個烏托邦連瞇著眼都看不到。

"They both weigh the same," the wandering witch said while pointing at the small and midsize hammer. "Choose one for your journey."

The little fox seemed to have learned his lesson. This time around he picked up the small hammer and went back to bridge building.

The small hammer didn't wear out, but the bridge it built was so tiny it couldn't reach the new utopia.

NEVER POOR

剛剛坐在橋墩上的巫女這時已經坐著掃帚飛到了小狐狸身後，一把抓起小狐狸的腰帶，像是拎菜籃那樣向前飛去。飛行的速度讓小狐狸睜不開眼睛，只聽見耳邊呼呼的風聲不斷吹過，接著風聲慢慢變小，巫女也慢慢的將小狐狸放到地上。巫女將最後一隻槌子給了他，然後帶著笑容消失在風中，這次倒是跟小狐狸的想像一樣。

　　小狐狸還是無法完全睜開眼睛，過了一下才發現前方有扇過度閃耀的黃金大門，門頂的刻字寫著「永不貧窮」。

The little fox was lucky though. The witch was heading in the same direction, so she took the little fox with her, handed him the midsize hammer, and dropped him off at a fancy golden gate. The inscription above the gate read "Never Poor".

不意外的，大門內仍然是一條充滿好奇心的超長隊伍，這次甚至多了一些焦慮的氛圍。這個烏托邦沒有太多的建築物，很容易看到隊伍終點座落著的黃金牧場，但奇怪的是視野所及之處沒看到任何動物。

　　「我沒有看到任何動物，」小狐狸向居民問到「你們排隊在等什麼呢？」

　　「我們在等著領金鵝幣。」

　　「這隻鵝很特別嗎？」

　　「金鵝幣不是動物，」另一個居民接著解釋「金鵝幣每天會生出另一個錢幣，那些錢幣隔一天也會再生出新的錢幣。」

　　小狐狸瞧了一眼背包裡那不知道是木屑還是麵包屑的殘渣，總之所剩無幾，雖然心裡還是有些疑問，但也默默的站到了隊伍末端。

　　The little fox again saw a long line of citizens, this time in front of a golden ranch, but curiously, no animal was in sight.

　　"I don't see any animals," said the little fox, "what are you lining up for?"

　　"A token goose," replied a citizen.

　　"What's so special about this goose?"

　　"It's not the animal itself," the citizen explained. "It's a token that breeds two more tokens every day, and those tokens do the same the next day."

　　The little fox looked at the meager breadcrumbs in his bag, thanked the citizen, and decided to queue up.

"Don't miss your chance, only 100 token geese available!." The most bizarre thing in this utopia was probably its citizens. Nothing about them was golden at all; they were so plain and ordinary it was confusing, as if hordes of people had marched into the planet from another dimension.

"100 token geese only, don't give it a second thought!" The crowds became increasingly agitated as the word spread, like an infectious disease ready to explode any time. The pushing and shoving of a few quickly turned into dozens of fights, which in turn erupted into skirmishes between hundreds of people. The street immediately fell into chaos, quickly wiping out any notions of order or civilization.

這個金黃色的烏托邦裡雖然建築物不多，但所有的人造物件都造的富麗堂皇。耀眼到讓人無法直視的黃金牧場自然不用多說，腳下的鋪石透著琥珀的光澤，路旁的秋葉似乎也比小狐狸以前所見過的更加閃亮。

　　「烏托邦就應該要長這樣。」自言自語的小狐狸忽然感覺到隊伍裡有些躁動。

　　「金鵝幣只有一百顆。」如果要說這個烏托邦裡有什麼格格不入，那大概就是它的居民們。金黃烏托邦的居民們一點也不金黃，他們樸素的令人困惑，就像是一整條進入了異世界的隊伍一樣，跟周遭形成突兀的對比。

　　「金鵝幣只有一百顆！」這個訊息在隊伍裡越傳越開，語氣也越來越激動。特別焦慮的居民讓自己走到更前面的位置，推了一把前面的人，前面的居民氣憤的反推了回來，第三個居民為了勸架也推了兩人一把，就像瞬間爆炸的傳染病一樣，幾個人的推擠馬上變成了十幾人的群架，十幾人的群架也快速變成了數百人的小型戰役，整條琥珀石路立刻亂成一團，什麼文明什麼先後早就拋諸腦後。

小狐狸一點也不強壯，但相較於不怎麼金黃的居民們他卻出奇地矮小，矮小到居民們的推擠像是遙遠上空發生的事。居民們爲了增加推擠力道而扎穩的馬步，反而爲小狐狸開出了一條褲襠山洞。既然路都開出來了小狐狸也不猶豫，一股勁兒地向前邁出步伐，不知不覺就走到了隊伍的最前端。

　　The little fox was not particularly strong, but compared to the not-so-golden citizens, he was remarkably small, so small that the pushing and shoving seemed more like stormy clouds violently drifting in the sky. The citizens did what they could to hit harder and avoid falling. With a wide stance, feet grounded in the floor, their legs formed a forest-like trail that the little fox didn't hesitate to cross, running with all his strength to reach the front of the line.

「我想要一枚金鵝幣！」即使其他居民都在忙著閃避彼此的巴掌，透明的小狐狸還是得用力揮手才能爭取到黃金國王的注意力。

黃金國王坐在高高的階梯頂端，身上無一處不覆蓋著金箔，小狐狸必須要同時瞇著眼睛跟扯開嗓門才能與國王對話。黃金國王的動作很慢，慢到小狐狸無法確認他是否聽到了請求，於是他踏上了階梯希望能縮短一點距離。

小狐狸發現自己多走一階國王的眉頭就多一層皺褶，手上的動作似乎也變快了。

「你能用金鵝幣買烏托邦裡的任何東西。」小狐狸連第三階的階梯都還沒碰到，黃金國王已經把金鵝幣丟了過來「好好享受你的財富。」接著他快速地揮了揮手示意小狐狸從側邊離開，揮手的速度之快連身上的金箔都有幾片掉到了地上。小狐狸識相的下了階梯，避開仍在彼此毆打的人群們，離開了黃金牧場。

"Can I have a token goose please?"
The wealth king, clad in gold, immediately pulled one out of his pocket. "You can buy anything with the tokens here," he promised.

"Enjoy your wealth," he added formulaically before turning to the next in line and repeating the sequence over again.

　　The little fox stared at his token goose for a whole day. Just when his eyelids couldn't get any heavier, the token symbol on his goose started to swell up. It seemed as if the goose was about to explode and then, two brand new tokens sprung up from behind it. The little fox bounced with such exhilaration he almost broke his bed.

小狐狸就這麼趴在床上盯著金鵝幣看了一整天，深怕錯過奇蹟。小狐狸的眼皮從來沒有這麼重過，他雖然時常焦慮地盯著天花板，但因為期待而硬撐著不睡覺這卻是第一次。就在他眼皮快闔起來的那一刻，金鵝幣開始如充氣般膨脹，本來還不到一個指節的金鵝幣現在卻跟小狐狸的手掌一樣大，錢幣上圓滾滾的鵝看起來瞬間懷了九月胎，雙頰也如貪心的天竺鼠一樣高高鼓起。

　　就在小狐狸覺得金鵝快要爆炸時，另一顆金鵝幣從背面蹦出，九月胎與天竺鼠瞬間消失。小狐狸興奮的拿著兩枚金幣在床上跳上跳下，幸好黃金做的床夠堅硬，不然兩枚金幣可能瞬間就得花光了。

不到幾天時間小狐狸已經成了富翁，他對自己感到滿意，甚至還買了條黃金褲來犒賞自己。但小狐狸也有了新的煩惱，他發現那些沒有拿到金鵝幣的居民們總在路上跟著他，一開始他並不介意這樣的關注，但時間一久心裡不免有些毛毛的。爲了解決問題他僱用了一名黃金侍衛，把他的財富放進了黃金寶庫，在陡峭的山丘上建了一座黃金碉堡，就是爲了離這些居民們遠遠的，他必須感受到安全。有一天他發現黃金衛士在偷看他的黃金畫作，就寫了一張黃金便條，通知他離職的黃金時段。

He amassed a fortune in just days. Then he began to notice that citizens who didn't get a token goose would follow him around. The little fox felt so uneasy he hired a golden guard, put his treasures in a golden safe, and built a golden fortress on top of a hill, far away from everyone. One day, the little fox caught the golden guard staring at one of his favorite golden paintings so he wrote a golden letter to fire him.

這陣子小狐狸覺得自己似乎過著夢想中的人生，一切都非常黃金，也相當順利。

但他跌倒了。這天他正在山丘的階梯上欣賞自己的黃金碉堡，想下個兩階看全碉堡的閃亮時，不小心踩了空。碉堡所建的山丘特別的陡，這也沒辦法，總不能讓那些跟蹤他的居民這麼容易接近他，但同個山丘也讓小狐狸的下墜速度越來越快，直到他重重的摔到了山丘腳才停下來。

小狐狸忍著無法忍受的疼痛抬起了頭，眼前的是當初的黃金牧場，現在牧場已經沒人在管了，如果仔細看似乎還能看到當初打鬥的痕跡。小狐狸想移動身體，但他發現自己的左手和右腳似乎都骨折了。他試著找人幫忙，但哪裡有人，連當初跟蹤他的人們都不見蹤影，他唯一能看到的是孤單陡斜的山丘上那些彼此離得遠遠的黃金碉堡們，互不相看、互不往來，只剩一片寂寞。

For a while, the little fox felt he was living his dream life in this hilltop utopia.

But then he fell hard. When admiring his fortress from the hillside stairs, he slipped accidentally and tumbled down to the bottom of the staircase. He struggled to lift his head up and gazed at the abandoned ranch. The pain was unbearable;—he had broken his left arm and right leg. He sought out help, but there was no one around, not even the people who used to follow him around. All he could see were shiny fortresses standing on lonely hilltops, far away from each other. Gone were the citizens, the lines, the fights. Only silence remained.

"Token geese aren't enough to make utopias," the little fox uttered as he teared up. "Not everyone is happy here."

He managed to grab some ropes from the ranch and tied the small hammer to his right ankle to be able to walk a bit. He gazed back at his golden fortress. It didn't seem as shiny as it used to be. Still, he had no color.

Injured and frustrated, the little fox left his second utopia.

「金鵝幣無法創造烏托邦，」小狐狸心情低落的說「不是所有人在這都是開心的。」

　　小狐狸拿了些牧場地上散落的繩子，將大小槌子綁上左手右腿，勉強支撐起身體。他抬起頭看了下自己建造的黃金碉堡，似乎也沒那麼閃耀了。小狐狸黯淡的離開了他的第二個烏托邦。

參考伊莉莎白鄧教授的研究與舊金山的城市發展，
對數位貨幣、去中心化金融、NFT、貧富差距問題的反思。
財富能帶來的快樂有極限，至少也不該用在建立黃金碉堡上。

.

Inspired by Professor Elizabeth Dunn,
Reflections on cryptocurrency, decentralized finance and NFTs
Remember that wealth can only bring you so much happiness and without
restraint, it can turn into a golden fortress.

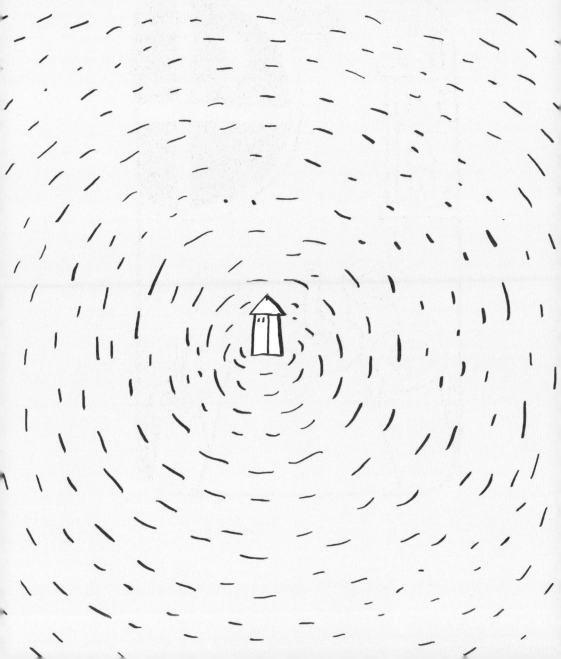

巫女略顯疲憊地降落在家門前的沙地上，她拍了拍身上因奔波而累積的灰塵，站直了修長的身子向家門走去。

　　沙地中間的小房子與其說是家，更像是某種鍛造的場所。外牆是用又大又方的灰白石頭砌成，除了正前方的木門和稍微從屋頂高起的煙囪之外，就沒有任何特別之處了。相較於巫女的家，沙地顯得相當寬廣，遠處有些土黃的樹叢，但並沒有帶來太多生氣，把距離拉遠了看，這絕對可以算是個渺無人煙的地方

The witch felt exhausted as she landed in the patch of sand in front of her house. Dusting off her clothes, she slowly managed to stand up straight and walked towards the door.

Lying amid the desolate patch of sand, the house resembled more a smithy than a home. Large, square stones in white and gray made up the walls, with nothing special except the wooden door in front and the protruding chimney on the roof. The patch of sand was quite spacious in comparison, with some yellowish trees in the distance. Nothing in the landscape exuded vitality whatsoever; this was a no man's land indeed.

Inside the small house was a small room, unexpectedly small, with furnishings of unexpected sorts. The walls of the house looked the same inside as out, dullish gray and white. There were only a few things in the room. Against the western wall lay a forge with the molds for three hammers of different sizes carved on top. There was no decoration to speak of. The witch's hammock was suspended from the roof of the eastern wall. Rather than a banana, its shape could be better described as a waxing crescent moon, slim and curved, as if tailor-made for the witch's figure. No matter the weather outside, no sunlight could seep in through the thick walls. Only silver light shimmered inside, like the dreamy reflection of moving water. Its source was the huge hourglass above the forge. The hourglass was as tall as the ceiling, but its bottom seemed to levitate above the ground. Its neck faced the forge, waiting to spill silver liquid from its inverted triangular shape.

Strictly speaking, this was not an hourglass, as it contained no sand. The silver liquid inside was not even ordinary water. It seemed to have a life of its own, constantly flowing without external interference. "Animated", that's what some would call it. Unfortunately, only about a quarter of the animated silver liquid remained in the hourglass now, and it continued flowing away slowly, drop by drop.

小房子裡不意外的是個小房間，意外的是房內的擺設。房子的內牆與外牆毫無兩樣，仍然是灰白一片。房間裡只有幾樣東西，靠著西牆的是一個鍛造爐，上面有著三種尺寸的槌子刻模，相當簡陋。東牆是巫女的吊床，吊床與其說是香蕉形狀，可能更像是初二的弦月，又細又彎，直直掛在天花板上，似乎是爲巫女身形量身定做的。外頭雖然頂著大太陽，卻沒有任何陽光能找到縫隙穿透灰白厚牆。內牆上只有銀色的光在躍動，像是在水裡波動一樣。銀色的光源是鍛造爐上方的巨大沙漏來的，沙漏的上方頂著天花板，下方卻沒踩著地，與鍛造爐接觸的是沙漏的束口處，倒三角形地等著把銀色液體漏入爐裡。

　　技術上來說，這大概不能稱作是沙漏，裡頭一粒沙也沒有，銀色液體也不像一般的水，看起來好像有生命一樣，在沒有外力的干擾下不斷四處流竄，用活潑形容可能恰到好處。可惜的是活潑的銀色液體現在大概只剩整個沙漏的四分之一高，而且還在緩慢卻持續地流失中。

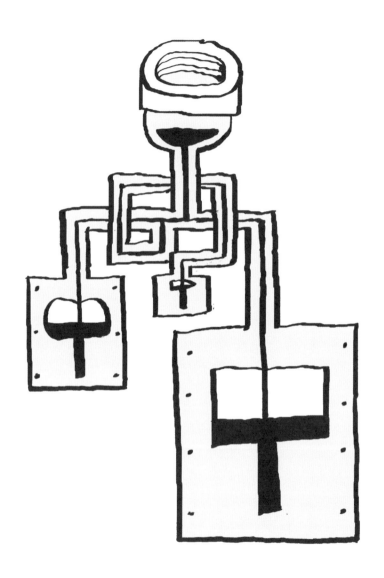

巫女修長的手正好能構到沙漏頂端，把不知道從哪搜集來的銀色液體由上方倒入沙漏中，手上的小瓶子一下就見底了，銀色平面完全看不出有任何起伏。巫女緊鎖著眉頭，看起來相當苦惱。

　　她接著打開了束口下端，銀色液體爭先恐後的分別流向三個大小不同的模子裡，瞬間就成了型。巫女將三隻定型的槌子從模子中拔起，看著最後一滴液體流光，房間也失去的唯一的光源。

　　The witch's slender hand could barely reach the top of the hourglass. In a vial, she had collected more of that silver liquid—no one knows from where—and was pouring it to replenish the hourglass. The vial emptied in an instant, but the silver surface remained still, as if nothing had happened. The witch furrowed her brow, looking very distressed.

　　She then opened the bottom of the neck, and the silver liquid speedily flowed into three differently- sized molds. It took shape in no time. The witch pulled the three resulting hammers out of the molds and saw the last drop of liquid flow away. The room descended into darkness.

烏托邦III

右角
Right Horn

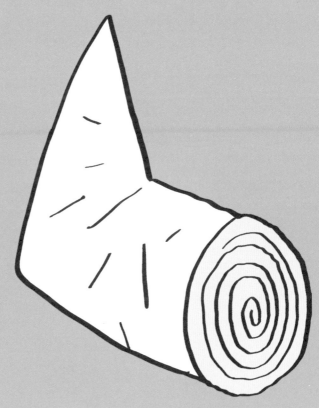

Once again, the bridge built by the little fox was embarrassingly tiny and didn't get him anywhere. What's more, the witch was nowhere to be found this time.

The little fox took out the midsize hammer. The abandoned ranch had plenty of wood he could use, so he built a wooden bridge.

小狐狸一跛跛沮喪地走出黃金烏托邦，遠方的迷你小橋還直直指著小狐狸，就像是在嘲諷他一樣。他轉頭四處望了望，巫女也不見了，小狐狸有點想念巫女，她的智慧總是讓他感覺到平靜。

　　他想起巫女離開前給了他最後一隻中槌子，中等的槌子有著剛好的重量，用起來很順手，敲起來既不像大槌子這麼空虛，也不像小槌子那麼狹隘，剛好附近散落了一些木材，於是小狐狸開始建造他的下一座橋。

There was a gate at the end, as usual.
The inscription above it read "Never stupid".

這次小狐狸的木橋建得方方正正規規矩矩，建完橋的槌子也完好如初。小狐狸看著橋覺得還算滿意，雖然心裡有些慾望沒被滿足，但自信心倒是拿回了一點。

　　不意外地，橋的終點是另一扇大門，這扇門的門框不用一般的磚塊搭，而是由上千本書籍堆砌而成，門頂的刻字這次寫著「永不愚蠢」。

"I'm not stupid." The little fox took it to heart.

He walked through the gate. Surprisingly, he found no line. "I guess no one likes to be called stupid,", he thought to himself.

「我才不愚蠢。」小狐狸對剛剛才重新找回的自信有點敏感，他帶著一絲憤慨的口氣對自己信心喊話，就像是哥哥站在欺負妹妹的惡霸身前一樣，維護著自己覺得重要的事物。他一跛跛地進了大門，跛的十分憤慨，深怕附近的陌生人也覺得他愚蠢。

　　奇怪的是這個烏托邦沒有任何的排隊人潮，只有洞見國王一個人悠然的站在街道中央。「我想大概沒有人想要被說愚蠢。」小狐狸發現街道兩旁全是書店，街道上的路人全拿著書，有人右手拿著咖啡，左手像特技般邊拿著書邊翻頁。也有人躺在書店門口的躺椅，讀了就睡，睡完再讀。如果書香真的是種氣味的話，這個香氣大概會在小狐狸的鼻頭繞個三天。

The insight king stood alone on the street, quite nonchalantly. He didn't seem worried about the fact that no one was rushing to get their hands on his gift.

This awakened the little fox's curiosity again. He approached the insight king and said, "I don't think I am stupid."

"Wait until you put these horns on." The horns were really weird-looking, one pointing up at the sky, the other drooping down. The insight king recognized the little fox as one of the most curious beings out there and the little fox wanted to make sure he's not stupid indeed, so he put on the two horns.

洞見國王的心情似乎沒有因為無人排隊而受影響，他在街道中央慢慢的來回散步，老舊卻不染塵的長袍後擺拖著街道吵吵作響，及胸的白色鬍鬚被他衰老的手指梳了一百多次，蚊子大概可以毫無障礙的順利穿越，他的眼神銳利，似乎看透一切，但也有點悲傷。

　　「我才不愚蠢。」走來的路上小狐狸在腦袋裡已經演練了五十次，還默默對自己舉了三個過去聰明的表現，他要堅定的告訴洞見國王，然後轉身就走，用力地為自己表達立場。

　　「試試看這雙角，如果到時你還是這麼覺得，我就相信你。」小狐狸連轉身都還沒完成就定住了，他看著乾皺雙手抓著的白色雙角，這兩隻角長的還真奇怪，一隻工整的直指天際，另一隻則扭曲成一個圓圈，尖角指向根部。小狐狸的不情願從來都不是好奇心和自尊心的對手，他從洞見國王手中接過雙角，就這麼戴上直指天際的左角，與直指腦門的右角。

小狐狸戴上雙角的瞬間就聽到國王沙啞的聲音，他聽著那些不斷重複的問題與公式，不是聽不懂的術語就是聽不懂的數學，有一刻他還懷疑國王是不是瘋了。他害怕的抬起頭看了國王一眼，但國王的嘴從一開始就沒動過，小狐狸這才發現自己聽的是洞見國王永不間斷的思緒，而其中有些問題，也許不要拿出來討論會好一些。

　　「我要拿這些問題怎麼辦？」

　　「你應該要⋯⋯」幾乎是同一時間小狐狸便從右角獲得了答案。應該說所有小狐狸腦裡的所有問題幾乎都在同一時間獲得了答案。

　　「太神奇了！」還好街邊的躺椅都已經躺滿了人，不然跳上跳下的小狐狸大概得對一些木頭和店家道歉。「我可以解決全世界的問題了。」愚蠢什麼的小狐狸早就不再在意，歡天喜地的連腳似乎都不那麼跛了。

　　Equipped with the horns, the little fox started to hear the king's voice, but the ruler had not opened his mouth even once. The little fox soon realized he was hearing the insight king's endless stream of thoughts from his new left horn. Among those thoughts, there were things that deeply troubled him.

　　"What do I do with the problems I hear?" Then another voice started coming out from the right horn. "Here's a solution…" Every question the little fox had was answered.

　　"How convenient!" The little fox thought, "Now I can solve all problems in the world!" No words could describe the enthusiasm he felt at the time.

在街上活蹦亂跳的小狐狸看起來特別突兀，尤其是他那雙奇怪的角，正常人看到他應該都會有意識的避開，免得受到怪異情況的波及。現在的小狐狸不但不愚蠢，他讓別人快樂的信念也十分堅定。長著雙角的狐狸開始聆聽烏托邦裡居民的問題，也出手幫忙。他幫腰痠的阿姨找到了按摩的祕密技巧，他幫絕望的大叔找回了愛上躲貓貓的貓，還幫男子調製了奪得書店老闆歡心的戀愛藥水，任何你想像到的事小狐狸都能幫忙解決。

小狐狸漸漸在烏托邦受到歡迎，雙角在居民的眼裡也不再怪異，有時候他們還會跟小狐狸借來戴一戴，解決一些他們不太好意思說出口的問題。小狐狸身上漸漸出現了顏色，走在路上竟然還有人跟他打招呼。

在小狐狸不自知的強力宣傳下，洞見國王來回散步的距離越來越短，身邊總是塞滿了人。但洞見國王表情還是一樣悠然，只是梳

The citizens tried to avoid the crazy fox roaming the streets. But he started helping them. He fixed doors, saved pets, resolved family problems, anything you can think of. As he solved difficulties for others, some color started to show on his fur.

All of a sudden, the horns didn't look so weird for people and citizens started putting these horns on their heads. The ones who did it first got them for free, but the king started asking for gold after a while.

鬍子的時間縮減了不少。洞見國王一開始還是免費分送了幾副角，但當雙角成爲烏托邦的風潮後，國王也開始收取金幣了。

Every horned citizen was now a problem solver, but they soon started finding the problems of regular citizens increasingly stupid.

One citizen broke off his left horn and stopped listening to others' minds. Many followed. They only wanted answers to their own problems. The newcomers with insufficient gold only bought right horns and not left ones.

Weeks after, no one was solving problems for others. Citizens who were not wealthy enough still had broken doors and faulty relationships. The horned citizens only talked to their own kind, and the rest of the citizens felt too scared to have a single thought.

那些有角的居民開始效法小狐狸，成爲問題解決專家。烏托邦在這樣的氛圍下似乎變得更加理想，可惜好景不常，很快的便有人開始認爲按摩或找貓這樣的任務實在太過低級愚蠢，自己也得不到任何好處，實在沒必要爲別人耗費精力。

　　一部分的雙角居民成了單角居民，他們把左角折成兩半，不再直指天際，也不再傾聽人心。單角居民們只想著解決自己的問題。剛接觸洞見國王的居民也因爲金幣不足，只買右角不買左角，畢竟自己的問題還是得先解決才行。

　　幾週過去了，除了小狐狸外，不再有人試著幫助別人解決問題，沒有金幣的居民們還是用著壞掉的傢俱，捧著痠痛的腰，也爲不值得的愛情大打出手。單角居民們成立了私人社團，買下了只讓單角居民進入的私人酒吧，短時間還開發了只給單角居民居住的私人社區。無角居民成了次級公民，雙角居民則讓所有人躲得遠遠的，不敢在他們附近產生任何想法。

「右角永遠是對的，但右角同樣不足以創造烏托邦。」看著烏托邦的三角對立，小狐狸慢慢開始對烏托邦失去信心。

　　這時他的左角又開始運作「國王午夜時都會在臥室裡更衣，我們趁那個時間點爬上城牆來取得王位⋯⋯」。

　　小狐狸心裡一陣淒涼，把拔下的雙角都折成兩半，放回背包。

Seeing the dysfunctional lives of the unhorned everywhere he went to, the little fox thought, "The right horn is always right, but these horns aren't enough to make utopias."

Through the left horn a voice uttered, "The insight king will be in his chamber by midnight. We'll climb up the window and take him down..."

Disheartened, the little fox broke off his left horn and decided to leave this utopia.

參考肖沙那、祖博夫教授的研究與知識科技潮流，

對資料監控及知識焦慮的反思。

資訊與知識都只是工具，窺視他人想法更是危險的使用方式。

Inspired by Shoshana Zuboff,
Reflections on data surveillance and knowledge anxiety
Information and knowledge are just tools,
and peeking into others' minds is a dangerous way of using them.

The friendship king finally arrived at the venue of the gathering. There, he saw the witch standing alone at the entrance. He remembered the witch's past kindness to everyone and greeted her with a nod and a grin. The witch's fatigue was yet more evident at this point, but still tried to smile politely in return.

The site for the kings' gathering was always chosen with utmost care and the center of the forest had received the honor on this occasion. A large portion had to be cleared in preparation. A giant round table made of the finest wood was placed in the very middle of this now open area. The tablet was so large that it took the friendship king ten minutes to walk to his seat. Despite its size, the table had only three seats, reserved for the kings only. The thrones were six times wider than the kings' buttocks and towered several feet above their heads. The friendship king sat down on his respective throne and swung his legs like a small child, but didn't seem to notice its sheer size. Instead, the expression on his face showed great contentment.

友好國王終於到達了開會地點，他看到巫女一個人站在入口旁，想起了巫女過去對眾人的恩惠，微笑著點頭示了示意。巫女這時候看起來似乎更疲倦了，但臉上仍試著掛著微笑，禮貌性的回了禮。

　　國王們開會的地點總是不能太隨便，他們大氣地把地點選在森林的正中央，特別開採出一塊大型空地，鋸下的木材全都用來打造開會用的超大型圓桌。讓我來形容一下超大型圓桌的意思，圓桌表面當然是上等木材的木紋，跟摯友工廠所用的木材質地相去不遠，但桌子的人小大概可以比擬任何廣場，友好國王走了十分鐘才走到自己的位置坐下。這個圓桌總共只有三張椅子，規定只有國王才能入坐，這些位子比國王們的屁股寬了六倍，椅背也比國王們的頭高出了好幾呎，友好國王上了座後就像是小朋友一樣，雙腳懸空的晃呀晃，但他好像沒有注意到椅子大小的不適，反倒露出了滿意的微笑。

Next, the golden king arrived. His entry was very pompous. Sheets of gold were scattered in anticipation of his every step to form a golden carpet. He also saluted the witch with a nod as he entered, then went on to draw a golden semicircle on the grass before sitting on his throne. He didn't notice the friendship king, who was too far away, and didn't greet him. The golden king's entrance was so flashy though; it soured the friendship king's mood a bit. He pretended nothing had happened, however, to avoid conflict.

Finally, the last monarch, the insight king, entered the venue. His throne was not far from the entrance so he took a seat before long. From far away, he heard the other two kings greeting him and he nodded to the other kings, who looked tiny sitting on their gigantic thrones. This made the two kings feel some sort of relief and they eventually started smiling again.

A wall covered in vines surrounded the entire round table. There was only a long, narrow gap at the entrance. The sun shone brightly on the table for most of the day, adding a sense of holiness to the place.

接著黃金國王也到了，散落的金箔成了他為自身鋪出的金毯，說有多氣派就有多氣派。黃金國王進場也向巫女點了點頭，在草地上繼續拖出三分之一圓的金色線條，因為友好國王坐的實在是太遠了，黃金國王連看都沒看見他，以至於也沒打招呼。但黃金國王的入場實在太招搖，友好國王默默地心裡不是滋味，但為了保持友好，也不好意思多說什麼。

　　最後一位洞見國王進場了，他的位子離入口處不遠，很快就能入座。但遠遠他就聽到兩位國王等著他打招呼的心聲，接著他便向那兩張大椅子上的小小國王們點了點頭，兩位國王也放下了心中的石頭，慢慢恢復了微笑。

　　巫女身後的背牆圍繞著整個圓桌，高聳的背牆爬滿了各式藤蔓，只有入口處是一條長長的細縫。大部分的白天時間陽光還是能很完整的直曬在桌上，一點也不顯陰暗，倒是增添了一點神聖感。

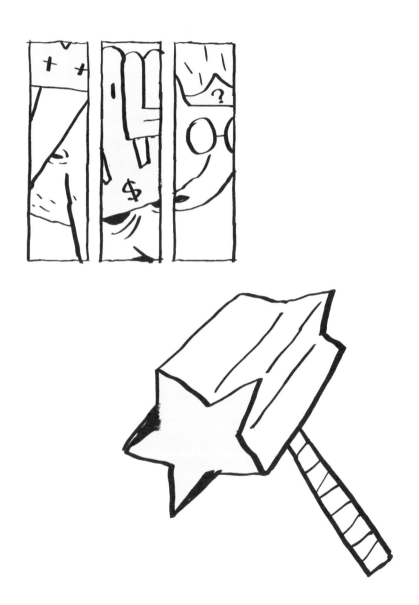

巫女飛到圓桌正中央，從背包裡拿出了剛鑄造好的三隻槌子，並用魔法提高了聲量。

　　「如果三位國王可以達成協議，各拿一支槌子回家，那這些創造新烏托邦的槌子就將屬於各位。如果你們無法達成共識，槌子就無法離開。」

　　國王們看起來有點緊張，他們都知道巫女法力無邊，特地召開國王會議來分發的槌子鐵定也不簡單，三人彼此猜忌甚至沒有注意到巫女已經從上方離開了大圓桌會議。

　　「我應該要拿最大的槌子。」洞見國王毫不猶豫的第一個出聲，「知識能創造最好的烏托邦，我能讓世界更加聰明。」

　　「我應該要拿最大的槌子。」黃金國王也不遑多攘，「錢財才能創造最好的烏托邦，我能讓世界更加富有。」

　　「我應該要拿最大的槌子。」友好國王一如往常謙讓的在最後發言，但也一如往常的少了點創意，「摯友能創造最好的烏托邦，我能讓世界更加友善。」

The witch flew to the center of the round table and took out the three hammers that had just been cast from her bag. She then launched a spell to raise the volume of her voice.

"'If you, three kings, can reach an agreement, each of you will be allowed to take a hammer back to your lands. These hammers will enable you to create new utopias to rule over. If you are unable to reach an agreement, however, the hammers will stay put. No one will be able to take them.'"

The kings looked a bit nervous. They all knew that the witch's magic was boundless and that the hammers brought to the gathering were invaluable treasures of incomparable power.

The three kings grew suspicious of each other, so much so that they did not even notice the witch hover and dart away from the gathering.

The insight king broke the tense silence and confidently proclaimed, "I should take the biggest hammer. Naturally, only knowledge can result in the best utopia. I can make the world smarter."

"'I should take the biggest hammer," The golden king quickly replied. "Wealth can create the best utopia. I am convinced that there will be no more poverty in the world."

The friendship king, spoke last, in a humble manner as always, "I should take the biggest hammer." Yet as always, he was a bit lacking in creativity. "The best utopia will surely be born from friendship. Peace will reign over the world."

An argument ensued. The insight king was determined to end the turmoil in his kingdom, so he climbed onto the table to snatch the biggest hammer. He turned and ran swiftly towards the door, but the entrance was blocked by the vines that stretched and intertwined to cover even the smallest crack on the walls. He turned and saw the other two kings chasing after him.

"The door has disappeared!" This, of course, failed to stop the kings from vying for the hammer. The chase that lasted for a few minutes turned into a clash that lasted for hours. The green leaves on the vines slowly yellowed. Their determination began to falter, but greed remained unabated. The golden king's sheets of gold were ripped and flew all over the place. The friendship king cast aside his ever-friendly guise. Tufts of the insight king's beard were pulled off. The kings' feet had long been numbed, but their gazes were equally fierce. The other two hammers still lay in the middle of the large round table, untouched by the disaster of their fight, as if dust felt ashamed of setting on them.

爭吵持續不斷，洞見國王決心要對抗國內的動亂，他爬上桌抓了最大的槌子，轉身便向門口飛奔。但原來的入口早已不在那了，兩旁的藤蔓快速的將高牆上的細縫堵住，他轉身一看，黃金國王跟友好國王雙雙追了上來。

　　「門消失了！」但這當然阻止不了國王們之間的爭搶，幾分鐘的追逐變成了幾小時的纏鬥，藤蔓上的綠葉慢慢開始泛黃，決心開始疲倦，貪心卻仍然貪心，黃金國王的金箔散得到處都是，友好國王早把友好拋諸腦後，洞見國王的鬍子也被拔掉了好幾撮。國王們的雙腳早就失去了知覺，但瞪著彼此的眼神還是一樣兇猛有力。另外兩隻槌子仍平擺大型圓桌中間，一點打鬥的灰塵也沒沾上，就好像碰了便是一種恥辱一樣。

「我要怎麼獲得力量並離開這個地方？」洞見國王忽然想到自己擁有無所不知的雙角。

「放下你手上的大槌。」腦中聲音不疾不徐地回答。

洞見國王感到很困惑，於是再問了一次。

「放下你手上的大槌。」這次的答案還是一樣。

洞見國王火上了頭，為什麼其他國王不能理解知識才是最重要的？他們憑什麼把雙角給弄壞？他們憑什麼觸碰他精心修剪的鬍子？他快速起身跑向原來門所在的位置，高高舉起大槌，用盡了全身的力氣往牆上敲去，期望能開出個洞讓自己離開。

高牆看不出有任何毀損，大槌子則完全粉碎，洞見國王握著的把手幾乎消失。洞見國王又驚訝又憤怒，顫抖的雙手加深了對巫女及其他國王的忿忿不平。他丟掉手上最後的鐵塊，忽然之間藤蔓開始移動，一整條陽光也切向會議桌。

三人對巫女的法力失去信心，想回到家的慾望也難以抑止，對另外兩個槌子看都沒看，就起身開始回程了。

The insight king suddenly remembered that he had those all-knowing horns and asked, "How do I gain strength and leave this place?".

"Put down the big hammer in your hand," the voice in his head uttered gravely.

The insight king felt bewildered, so he repeated the question.

"Put down the big hammer in your hand," the voice retorted invariably.

The insight king became angry. Why couldn't the other kings understand that knowledge was the most important thing? How dare they damage his horns? How dare they ruin his carefully trimmed beard? He quickly stood up and ran to the door's original location. He lifted the big hammer high and pounded it against the wall with all his strength, hoping to open up a crack.

The high wall was left unscathed, but the hammer fell into pieces. Down to its handle, almost all of it disintegrated in the insight king's hand. Rage and horror filled his heart. His hands trembled as his resentment towards the witch and the other kings grew deeper and stronger. He threw away the last piece of iron still in his hold and, suddenly, the vines began to move and a beam of sunlight shone on the table.

The three kings lost faith in the witch's magic and grew eager to return to their kingdoms. Without even looking at the other two hammers, they stood up and set out on their journeys home."

對世界政府在氣候變遷談判及進展的失望。

有時候就只是退一步這麼簡單。

Disappointment with the progress of governments worldwide
on climate change.
Sometimes it's just as simple as taking a step back.

烏托邦 IV

大千戲院

Theaterland

    After three failed attempts, the little
fox started to feel he was on the wrong
track.

    "What makes utopias?

    And how can I build a bridge that's
good enough?"

    The wooden bridge was useful, but it was not what the little fox wanted. It
bored him.

    He needed something more exciting, a slightly larger hammer, yet not so
unwieldy that it'd fall apart.

    He looked at the horn he'd just broken off from the top of his head. It
didn't weigh much, but attaching it to the hammer did the job.

    With a slightly larger hammer, the little fox's dreams grew a bit bigger as
well. He built a bridge out of ivory, the material the horn was made of. He
felt thrilled. It was amazing.

小狐狸現在已經經歷三個烏托邦了，他開始反省自己是不是搞錯了什麼？

　　「烏托邦應該要長什麼樣子？」烏托邦既不友善，也不黃金，更沒有長角。

　　「怎麼才能建座好橋？」木橋很實際，但小狐狸似乎無法從中獲得滿足，總覺得有點無趣、毫無新意。他需要一些刺激，也許是一個稍微大一點的槌子，他當然不是不記得教訓，「只要大一點就好。」至少敲擊的扎實感還是得在。

　　他掂了掂才剛折斷的雙角，沒什麼重量，而且正好可以接上槌子的兩端。

　　新槌子雖然不是深思熟慮的結果，但哪些成功不靠些緣分呢？槌子大了點，小狐狸的夢想跟野心也稍微大了一點。象牙白的槌子敲出了一座象牙白的橋，不像木頭這麼無聊，也沒有黃金這麼造作，小狐狸為自己的突破感到興奮，高亢的情緒為眼神充了電，直直望向下一個烏托邦。

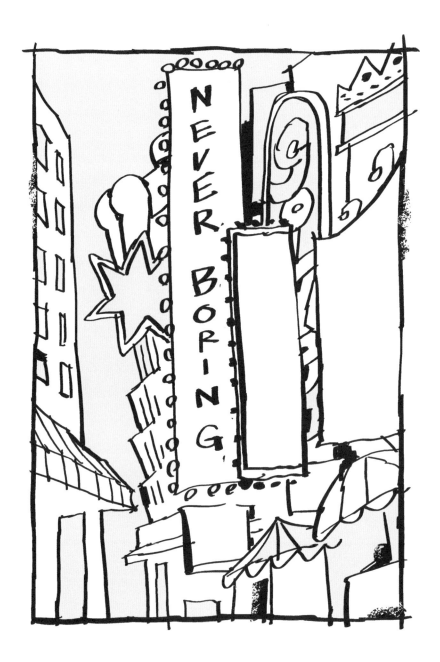

這次的大門比小狐狸的眼神還要絢麗，門框上掛滿了各種顏色的燈，與其說是門，可能更像是棵聖誕樹。這些燈光在白橋上也映射出了多道彩虹，溫馨地向小狐狸表達歡迎之意。

　　門上的刻字也是霓虹燈排成的，老實說得花點時間讓眼睛習慣一下這些五光十色，才能看清上面寫了什麼。

　　「永不無聊」的永字上方那一點不斷閃爍，不是燈壞了，而像是故意吸引大家注意的小動作。小狐狸才剛建了座不無聊的白橋，霓虹刻字正好對了他的胃口，他已經準備好面對他的下一次探險了。

At the end of the ivory bridge he found a gate as before. The inscription above read "Never Bored". The little fox felt proud of his accomplishment, the ivory bridge, and he was ready to go after some more excitement.

He sensed the festive mood as soon as he stepped through the gate. There were at least a hundred performers welcoming people into their theaters.

"What is this place?"

"This, young man," one of the performers answered, "is the utopia of a thousand theaters."

"Where's your king?" The little fox asked.

"We don't need a king, darling," a woman with a heavy coating of makeup on her face answered. "We have stars."

一踏進大門，慶典的氣息便席捲而來，夾道歡迎的不是居民，而是打扮華麗的舞者與演員，他們每個都對著小狐狸獻上最溫暖的微笑，小狐狸的嘴角沒有選擇，只能自然上揚。

　　「這是什麼地方？」

　　「年輕人啊，」較為年老的演員對著他說「這是擁有上千戲院的烏托邦。」

　　「你們的國王在哪裡呢？」小狐狸不確定自己是否聽懂了老演員的回答，於是就繼續問下去。

　　「親愛的，我們沒有國王，」那個妝化得最濃的舞者接著說「我們只有閃耀的明星。」

小狐狸繼續走在這條讓人眼花撩亂的街道上。劇院們用力爭奇鬥豔，有些讓招牌大放煙火，另一些讓劇名像蛇一般在空中竄動，有些發出雷聲般的巨響，另一些則用迷魂的香味吸引客人，全都是為了讓小狐狸走進門裡。小狐狸對於誘惑的抵抗力明顯不高，他只想著這輩子再也不會無聊了，五花八門的選擇讓小狐狸暈頭轉向，他像那些芭蕾舞者一樣開始原地轉圈，到了第十三圈甚至還聽到了銅板落地的聲音，但不管他轉得再快，都跟不上大千戲院的歡樂節奏。

　　大千劇院的亮點當然是永遠看不完的劇場，無論你何時出現在街上，都有全新的劇本和更高的飆音在等著。小狐狸自從進入這個烏托邦後就沒有停下腳步，馬拉松式的走遍了所有劇場，然後再發現自己實在跟不上劇場戲碼的更新速度。鼓掌的雙手已經完全麻痺，但劇場實在太過精彩，放下雙手實在是對不起那些盡心盡力的演員舞者。

　　The little fox continued treading on this flamboyant avenue. Neon signs were ubiquitous and not a second went by without music and dancing.

　　Live shows ran constantly at every theater. Filled with amazement, the little fox entered one venue after another, tirelessly clapping, moved by the stories presented in each single show.

「那是蕾拉，」小狐狸的世界不再大千，也不再快速運轉，他的時間好像就停在了一個點上。他抽不了身，也無法抽身，「她是最棒的。」跟小狐狸靜止在同一個時空的觀眾說道，他們的對話沒有任何的眼神交會，即使是一秒鐘，他們也不願意把眼神從蕾拉身上移開。

　　蕾拉藏青色的長裙下露出赤裸的雙腳，美得像吉普賽人那樣自由奔放，也美得像天神貴族一般雍容優雅。她唱歌從來沒有配樂，沒有音樂配得上她的歌喉，她一開口全場便屏氣聆聽，深怕自己的呼吸聲干擾了天籟的完美。她跳舞從來無需燈光，觀眾炙熱的眼神總是把舞台照得燈火通明，多半盞燈都會讓蕾拉顯得過度耀眼。蕾拉讓人窒息，讓人盲從，小狐狸自然也不例外。

　　Then something caught his eyes. "That's Lela," a member of the audience sitting next to him said while continuing to stare at the stage, "isn't she dazzling?" "Very," the little fox replied. Their eyes never met as they conversed. Their hearts were captivated by the woman on stage.

As time went by, the little fox followed Lela everywhere. He knew every role she played, every line she said, and every song she sang.

He wanted to see Lela. He craved to meet her in person, to figure out how she managed to look so stunning everyday and resonate so well with every soul. More than anything, he wanted to be let in on her secret — how was she able to make everyone laugh and cry and look so colorful all the time?

So he waited at the exit after every show. Days and nights went by but she never showed up. He only saw an old man cleaning and walking out the exit.

蹲在戲院裡的小狐狸早就失去了對時間的掌控，他不知道已經過了多少白天、多少黑夜，他只知道自己得跟著蕾拉走。小狐狸能覆誦蕾拉的每一句台詞，預測她每一步舞步，也深深同理蕾拉扮演的每個角色，就算如此，他還是會在蕾拉的表演中流淚。

他希望能見見蕾拉，他必須要見到蕾拉，他必須知道蕾拉為何能如此超凡脫俗，卻又能夠共鳴人心。他希望知道蕾拉是如何一張嘴讓人嚎啕大哭，一伸手又讓人破涕為笑，又為什麼她總是那麼光彩奪目，她的顏色到底從何而來？

小狐狸每次表演結束便守在舞台的出口，就盼著蕾拉能從出口出現讓他問幾個問題。十場表演過去了，二三十場表演也都過去了，蕾拉從來都沒有出現過，小狐狸唯一見過的只有秀後彎著腰在一旁打掃的老人。

He waited patiently. He didn't want to be abrupt, much less scare Lela, but after a while he just couldn't keep the question to himself anymore.

"Where's Lela?" he asked the old man as he came out of the stage exit. The old man didn't bat an eye.

"I waited here everyday just to get a chance to talk to her."

The old man stood quiet. He laid down his backpack and removed the cover. There was Lela.

The little fox was confused. Why was Lela carried around in a bag? Why were her limbs bent in weird ways with strings attached to them?

小狐狸很有耐心，他當然不想嚇到蕾拉，也不想給蕾拉奇怪的印象。但這麼多日子過去了，他實在按耐不住，於是他開口詢問了老人蕾拉的去向。

　　「請問蕾拉在哪？」彎腰老人還沒來得及把後台的門給鎖上，小狐狸就衝了上去，低著頭的老人沒有看向小狐狸，他只是拉了拉自己的帽沿，繼續把門給鎖好，以免有奇怪的觀眾跑進後台。

　　「我每天都在這裡等她，只希望能跟她講上一句話也好。」小狐狸快要哭出來似的，聲音帶了點哽咽，也帶了些絕望。

　　老人沉默地繼續彎著腰，右手抓向側邊的大袋子，放在小狐狸身前。大袋子看起來很重，也難怪天天背著它的老人腰會彎成這樣。老人翻開了上層的帆布，映入眼簾的是小狐狸熟悉的藏青色，不熟悉的則是眼前的怪異景象。

　　為什麼蕾拉會在一個大帆布袋裡？為什麼蕾拉的四肢彎曲的角度如此怪異？為什麼她身上有這麼多的鋼線纏繞？

Lela was a puppet. The old man picked up a pair of her backup puppet eyes and handed them to the little fox. "Thank you for your support," he said.

The old man put Lela back into the bag and walked away, leaving the little fox alone and broken.

The little fox felt his color dim again, but that's ok, he didn't want to be seen anymore.

蕾拉是個木偶。

　　彎腰老人的手在帆布袋裡撈來撈去像是在找些什麼，最終將手攤在小狐狸面前，手上是蕾拉的一雙備份眼睛。老手向前多遞了一下示意小狐狸將閃耀的雙眼收下。

　　「謝謝你的支持。」老人將蕾拉的手腳再度收進帆布袋中，把大袋子扛上肩便離開了，只剩下破碎的小狐狸留下。

　　小狐狸感覺他的顏色幾乎要完全消失，但也沒什麼關係，他也不想再被誰看見了。

對網紅、追蹤經濟、數位娛樂的反思。
別迷失在遙不可及的關係中，兩邊都是。

Reflections on internet influencers, follower economy,
and entertainment streaming platforms
Don't get lost in relationships that are out of reach,
no matter what side you're in.

對國王們來說，他們的家即使不叫面目全非，大概也已經完全認不出來了。

友好的街道現在充滿暴力。黃金廣場像是鬼城一般，連個影子都找不到。洞見城堡正在被政變侵蝕。這些已經不再是國王們的烏托邦了。

巫女飛過各個烏托邦上方，臉上的笑容已經被憂愁抹去。她看到洞見國王無所不知的雙角現在只能緊急地用來回答下一個安全的藏身處在哪。她看到黃金國王拿著一袋袋金幣走遍各個山丘央求居民們回來重建黃金烏托邦的經濟。她看到友好國王鼻青臉腫的勸架，永遠擋不住往身上招呼的拳頭。

The kings were entirely unable to recognize their kingdoms now.

Violence was now rife on the friendly streets. The golden town square had turned into a ghost town. Insight castle was shaken by a coup. These were no longer the utopias of the kings.

The witch flew above each utopia. A grimace of sorrow now replaced her smile. She saw how the insight king's all-knowing horns were now only being used to urgently seek the next shelter. She saw the golden king treading heavily through the hills with bags of golden geese, begging the citizens to return to rebuild the golden utopia and its economy. She saw the friendship king, his nose and face swollen from the punches he endured as he desperately attempted to plead with his people.

The witch had a secret that she had kept away from everyone. Her magic was always full of power and wonder, yes, but the source of her magic was not endless and had already been depleted. The hammers made for the king's gathering were her last hope, where she had used the last drop of her silver liquid. Even worse, not only her magic would vanish with the liquid, she would perish too.

She waved her hand gently, tears filling her eyes as she saw the world she'd helped create. She fell from the sky like a bird that had lost her wings, silently and unnoticed, plummeting across layers of clouds. A sentence could be read on the sky, in silver, after her fall:

"We must build a road for everyone together."

OUR OWN PATH

　　巫女有個從沒告訴別人的祕密，雖然她的魔法一向充滿力量與驚奇，但魔法的來源卻並非無窮無盡，其實早已見底。這次爲了國王會議所製作的槌子便是她用盡銀色液體所寄託的最後希望。當銀色液體流乾後，巫女的魔法會消失，巫女也將不復存在。

　　她看了看這個她幫助創造的世界，向空中揮了一揮手，便像失去骨頭支撐一般從高空的掃帚落下，沒有聲音，也沒有人注意到，默默地落進了遠方的雲層中。唯一留下的只有天空中的大型銀色句子。

　　「我們得一起打造大家的路。」

從格倫、威爾與唐鳳的多元主義得到靈感。

合作堆疊勝過零和競爭。

Inspired by Glen Weyl & Audrey Tang's new book on plurality.
Collaboration is more constructive than zero-sum competition.

門前的精靈

Genie at the Gate

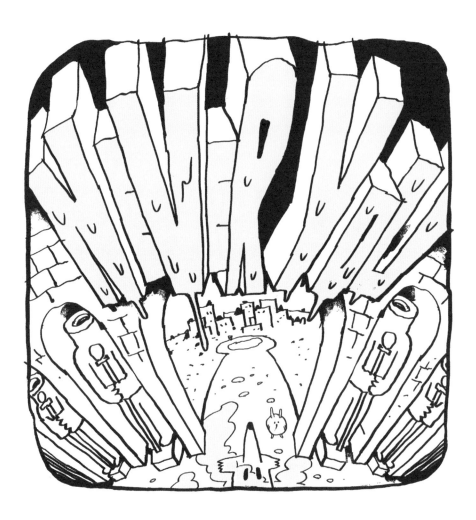

小狐狸的生氣像是被吸乾了一樣，顏色透明到無法分辨小狐狸是否還真的存在。小狐狸站在霓虹的門外，對於接下來該做些什麼毫無想法。他的手自己動了起來，做了他唯一知道怎麼做的事，他繼續造橋。

　　這次的白橋同樣精緻，但美得黯淡了些、哀傷了點。小狐狸失去了對烏托邦的興趣，失去了讓人快樂的動力，也失去了對自己的信念。但世界沒有因此停下，另一扇門還是出現在小狐狸的面前。

　　這次大門旁站了一位圓滾滾的矮小精靈，他專心地追著自己用魔法變出來的蝴蝶。如果不是那隻蝴蝶從小狐狸身前飛過，讓精靈直接撞上小狐狸空蕩的軀殼，矮小的精靈大概永遠不會發現小狐狸的存在。

　　倒在地上的精靈摸了摸自己紅腫的鼻頭，決定先做個自我介紹。

　　「我是精靈，在這個烏托邦裡我可以幫你完成一個願望。」

　　小狐狸抬頭一看，刻字寫著「永不是你」。

It seemed as if life had been sucked out of the little fox. Utterly clueless about what to do, he got back to what he was good at.

He built another bridge, this time a little gloomy, a little sad, but still beautiful in its own way.

The little fox was losing faith in utopias. He was losing faith in his original mission. He was losing faith in himself.

A gate appeared as always, but this time there was a genie guarding the gate.

"Who are you?" The little fox asked coldly.

"I am a genie. I'm here to grant you a wish before you enter."

The little fox looked up. The inscription above the gate read "Never You".

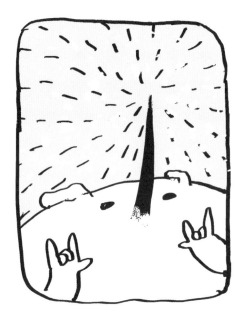

The little fox stared at the two words and thought about the things he hated about himself.

He hated being colorless. He hated that Lela was just an illusion. He hated the fact that he could do nothing to make himself or others happy. Perhaps if he was not himself, if he was someone exuberant and colorful instead, maybe then, things would be easier.

"I wish I was red," the little fox wished. "You know, the color of foxes."

The genie nodded and repeated the wish, "This little fox wishes to be red".

"You will get what you wished for as soon as you walk past the gate", the genie proclaimed.

The little fox felt a spark of hope light up again.

小狐狸盯著這四個字許久，「永不是你」提醒了他如何痛恨自己。他恨自己這麼透明、他恨蕾拉只是個幻覺，他恨自己沒有辦法讓任何人開心。他恨自己沒有朋友、沒有財富、沒有知識、沒有光芒、沒有顏色、也沒有存在。

　　如果他有了顏色，也許一切就會不同。

　　「我希望我是紅色的，」小狐狸說出了他的願望。「就是狐狸應該要有的顏色。」

　　渾圓的精靈前後搖動了一下表示理解，重複著說「狐狸希望自己是紅色的。」

　　「踏進門的那一瞬間，願望就會達成。」小狐狸聽著精靈的話，只期望逃避現在的自己，他實在不想再做小狐狸了。

小狐狸走進門就發現了一個完全不一樣的世界。

傳說裡的飛龍與鳳凰在天空飛舞，獨角獸在各處拉起了彩虹，到處都豎立著魔法尖塔，所有居民似乎都擁有自己的城堡，每個王子都有公主可以救，每個公主也都有著自己的冒險故事。

「原來人人如願以償的世界是長這個樣子。」

接著他看了看自己的手背，他不再是透明的小狐狸了。溫暖柔順的紅色毛髮覆蓋著他的皮膚，光是摸著就能起到安撫療癒的作用。他找了一面鏡子，然後不斷的做出奇特的動作來確認鏡中的人就是自己。濃密的毛髮不管再怎麼撥都是紅色的，他還拔下一小撮放進背包裡作爲紀念。

As soon as he walked past the gate, he saw a different world.

There were dragons and unicorns, magic towers and castles, noble knights and fair princesses. "So this is the world where everyone gets what they want."

Then he took a look at himself. No longer was he colorless, invisible. He had red fur, just like a proper fox.

他不再懷疑自己的毛髮是眞是假，放下戒心的同時眼淚也蹦的一聲彈了出來。過去這段時間小狐狸不知道哭了多少次，只有這次的眼淚是快樂的，他終於得到了他夢寐以求的顏色，他終於可以做完整的自己。

完整的自己？聽起來似乎有點抽象，但誰在意呢？只要他是紅色的就好了，不是嗎？

小狐狸四處奔跑著交新朋友，被現實吸乾的生氣已經全部回到他體內，他現在有著充沛的能量和高漲的情緒，再也沒有人忽略他，他現在是個正常的狐狸了。

The little fox burst into tears. He'd finally gotten what he has always wanted. He felt complete now.

"Complete?" It sounded vague somehow, but that didn't matter because he was a red fox now.

The little fox went about and made friends. He was full of life. No one was ignoring him anymore. He was "normal".

這完美的結局並沒有持續太久，小狐狸忽然發現他的背包變得很輕，打開後他發現他之前留下的金鵝幣都消失了。

　　「一定有人許了想要全世界財富的願望，」他的一個新朋友跟小狐狸解釋著「這個願望挺頻繁的。」小狐狸心一冷，想著沒錢晚上要怎麼填飽肚子，對這完美的世界也開始有了不好的預感。

　　Everything seemed perfect… until it wasn't. All of a sudden, the little fox felt his bag become lighter. He opened it and found all the tokens from before were gone.

　　"Someone must have made a wish to have all the money in the world." One of his newly made friends said, "That's a common one."

　　The little fox couldn't believe what he was hearing. Was there something imperfect about this world?

Again his bag lost more weight. The right horn attached to his hammer was gone. "Someone must have made a wish to have all the knowledge in the world."

The little fox felt dismayed. He kept looking at his bag to see what else was missing.

"What in the world is going on here? This is outright stealing!" He turned to ask his new friends and realized that they were gone too. Someone must have made a wish to have all the friends in the world.

接著他的背包又變輕了，槌子上的右角現在也消失了。

「一定有人許了想要全世界知識的願望。」

小狐狸還沒反應過來，背包裡的物品就一件一件接著消失。他既氣憤又焦急，只能死死地盯著背包深處看還有什麼東西在消失。

「這到底是怎麼一回事？這是偷竊！」他激動地轉身想跟他的朋友問清楚，才發現朋友們也已經消失。

一定有人許了想要全世界朋友的願望。

對元宇宙數位經濟的反思。

資源永遠是稀缺的，我們只是需要找到好方法分享而已。

Inspired by metaverse forecasts and understanding.
Reflections on building digital worlds with real economy.
Resources will always be scarce, so we must find better ways to share them.

不存在的烏托邦

Utopia is No Place

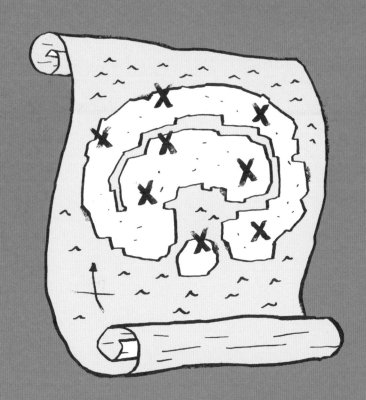

小狐狸幾乎失去了所有，也包括了他的顏色。最完美的世界最後變成了最可怕的噩夢。

「沒有哪裡是烏托邦。」

小狐狸帶著絕望的心情走出大門，「永不是你」四個字似乎打算永遠嘲笑小狐狸的天真與愚蠢，追逐蝴蝶的精靈早就不在那兒了，夜晚看起來比平常更加黑暗。

小狐狸再也不想去更多的烏托邦了，他甚至開始對巫女產生了一點怨恨，如果不是她的建議，小狐狸也不必經歷這麼多痛苦。「只要躲在狐狸村就可以了。」畢竟沒有期待哪來的傷害。他坐在門旁的大石頭上等著被拯救，心裡的無助早就超過可以承受的界線，幾個小時他都像石化般動也不動。

The little fox lost almost everything, even his color. What seemed like the most perfect world turned out to be the worst.

"Utopia is no place."

Desperate, the little fox crossed the gate to return outside. The words "Never You" seemed to mock him. The genie was no longer there. The world seemed dark and hopeless.

The little fox didn't know where to go next, certainly not another utopia. He sat on the rock where the genie previously stood. The little fox wished so badly that someone would save him. The crushing weight of helplessness was unbearable. He rolled back and lay there prostrate for hours. The sun was about to rise as he started to hear things.

不多久，微微升起的日出打破了黑夜的沉默，小狐狸似乎可以聽到遠方的一些聲音。

聲音的距離太遠，小狐狸聽不見也看不清遠方正在發生什麼事。他低頭看了一下背包裡還剩下的物品：折成兩節的左角、摯友的微笑、還有心愛蕾拉的眼睛。創造些什麼大概是小狐狸唯一可以逃避痛苦的方式。他拿起了這些物品開始互相拼湊，不多久竟然給他拼湊出了一副望遠鏡。

兩節直挺挺的左角成了望遠鏡的兩隻管身，好像還有點收音的作用。蕾拉閃耀的雙眼則成了目鏡鏡片，額外附帶了一些照明的功能。摯友的微笑成了連結雙管的對焦輪，笑得越開朗，看得就越遠。

The voices came from far away and he couldn't make anything out of them. The little fox looked inside his bag again. Only a couple of objects remained: the left horn broken in half, his wooden friend's smile, and Lela's backup eyes.

Even in the bleakest of times, the little fox got up and decided to build. He somehow managed to make a telescope with these objects. The pieces of the broken horn acted as tubes connected by the wooden smile. Lela's beautiful eyes became the front and back lenses. He was now able to see where the voices came from.

Through the telescope, he saw the insight king and the friendship king gathered on the tiny bridge. They were striking a deal regarding left horns, so that citizens of the best friend utopia would listen to real opinions.

He spotted on the wooden bridge the best friends migrating to the wealth utopia, hoping to keep the owners of token geese company at their hilltop fortresses, without them having to worry about theft.

He noticed some token geese accidentally dropped by travelers on the ivory bridge. It made everyone in the insight utopia slightly richer. Everyone was able to afford horns and became equal at last.

The little fox also observed his old best friend crossing the bridge to the land of a thousand theaters, dreaming to become the next Lela.

Were his eyes playing tricks on him? The little fox seemingly caught a glimpse of some silver sparks glittering on the bridge.

小狐狸拿著望遠鏡向發聲處望去。

　　小狐狸看到了他建造的小橋上，洞見國王正和友好國王兩人正面對著面，用怪異的單腳站立姿勢與對方談話。他們正在約定借用大批左角，讓友好烏托邦的居民可以多聽聽別人的真實意見。

　　小狐狸看到了他建造的木橋上，一整群的摯友們正在移民到黃金烏托邦，希望能給居住在陡峭山丘上、黃金碉堡裡的居民們一些陪伴，而且不用擔心任何偷竊的問題。

　　小狐狸看到了他建造的白橋上，有著一兩顆因為旅行而掉落的金鵝幣，這些幣讓洞見王國的居民們都有了買角的錢，讓烏托邦裡的人們可以更平等的對話。

　　小狐狸看到他的老摯友跨越了三座橋到了大千戲院的烏托邦，夢想著成為下一位蕾拉。

　　不知道是不是小狐狸眼花，他似乎看到這些橋上閃耀著一些銀色的火花。

　　　　　　　　　　　　　　　　　　　　結局　不存在的烏托邦

小狐狸又在石頭上多坐了一陣子，久到可以看到友誼的開始、爭吵的結束、也許還有些奇蹟的發生。

　　小狐狸現在懂了，不管是什麼樣的烏托邦，居民總歸都是人，而人總是破碎且有缺點的。

　　沒有哪裡是烏托邦，但只要我們持續造橋，一切都會沒事的。

　　小狐狸還是透明的，但現在看起來更像顆閃耀的鑽石。

The little fox sat on the rock for a bit longer, long enough to see friends bonding, quarrels ending, and miracles taking place.

He realized that no place is an utopia, because we're all broken.

Yet if bridges are built, we can always expect a better tomorrow.

No place is an utopia, and that's okay.

He was still a colorless fox. His fur might not have turned any color, but it shone like a diamond.

Story inspired by
Antoine de Saint-Exupéry's The Little Prince,
which brings humanity back to everything.
Thomas More's Utopia,
which taught us that even if utopias don't exist, there's a purpose for it.
Parsons GEMS V, which made this possible.
My parents, who always encouraged me to be good.
And my grandma, thank you for your time with us.

靈感來自
安托萬迪・聖修伯里的《小王子》、
湯瑪斯・摩爾的《烏托邦》、
帕森設計學院全球高管學程、
以及我的父母，永遠推動我做個好人、
還有過世的奶奶，謝謝妳的陪伴。

　　　　　　　　　　　　　　　結局　不存在的烏托邦

2023 限時

掃描 QRCODE 領取
烏托邦出席證明 NFT

現實世界的烏托邦們

　　乍看之下《迷航烏托邦》似乎是個友情故事，但友情的重要性已被包裝過千萬次，故事、漫畫、電影，如果想要創造些新的事物，友情似乎不是最好的題材。再說了，如果要講友情的話，對於朋友角色的刻畫可能還得更深一點，友情並不是《迷航烏托邦》想要討論的主題。

　　在科技業裡也打滾了快二十年，我的恆常大概就是不斷追逐些新可能。像小狐狸一樣，我的性格也有著缺陷，但若不是這些缺陷，我今天大概也不會寫這本書。這些新科技、新可能、新技術永遠都有著宏大的理想願景，它們創造新的生態系、商業模式，最終也創造新的財富階級。每個科技帝國（或聯邦）都承諾理想國度、經濟奇蹟，有時他們承諾實現我們的貪念或痴迷，另一些時候承諾減低我們的恐懼或焦慮，我們像小狐狸一樣因人性缺陷而被轉換，規模化的情緒支配也成了完整的學科。創業者像信眾一樣在其中追逐成功與財富，我們以爲在追求世界大同，結果通常卻只加深了階級隔閡。我支持科技進步，我也會持續在新領域裡創新，但如果科技產業是爲人類大同設計的工具/產品，那目的不應該只是創造個人財富或地位，而是創造更多連結的橋樑。

其實創作的過程並不是太複雜，我先歸納了一些常見的「科技承諾」，再將兌現這些承諾的執行問題給移除，將科技承諾的完成度推往極限，很快就可以看到現實與理想的差距，這個方式一點也不難，誰都可以這樣做。你們跟承諾互動的時候也許也可以試試看這個方法，也許能找到更多新奇的故事與角度。

像是前文講的，故事裡的烏托邦都影射著某類型的科技帝國，說得更精準點，我並不是在單指哪些企業或組織，而是泛指會做出那些「永不」承諾的組織或科技明星們。「Never Poor」、「Never Stupid」、「Never Alone」都是在形容恐懼，如果你學過科技業曾經流行且廣泛採用的遊戲化技巧，那你可能知道恐懼是人類最強大的短期驅動力，科技新創在追求成功的時候大概也無法不使用這些暗黑魔法。

每個烏托邦的結局大多有相關研究結果支持，以「永不孤單」

為例，麻省理工學院的教授雪莉特克爾 2012 年曾經出版過一本書叫《Alone Together》，書的副標是 Why We Expect More From Technology and Less from Each Other。其中部分重點是在講述我們在希望獲得安慰或是與人創造連結時，一般人都有兩個選擇，一是找人面對面談話，二是在社群網站上貼文。你會選擇哪一個？面對面談話能夠更直接地獲得對方的語氣與肢體回饋，但這些回饋不總是百分百正面，而我們很常為了逃避這樣的不確定性，而選擇貼出只有點讚選擇的貼文，同時還能獲得大量支持的幻覺。但實際上點讚創造的連結非常地弱，很難彌補我們內心對與人連結的真正需求。相反的面對面深度交談更能真正連結人們，但卻因為進入門檻高而常被選擇放棄。近年也有更多數據形容這個趨勢的惡化，日本年輕人戀愛的比率越來越低，從草食轉為絕食，越親密的關係經驗率的下滑就越劇烈，這正是選擇較為輕鬆與人工的人際關係的結果。小狐狸在書中的摯友可以代表任何一種科技，社群網站、AI 友情、甚至是紅了一陣的計時陪伴服務，都是我們逃避學習與人建立真實關係的選項。

　　「永不貧窮」的黃金烏托邦講的是我所在的，吵吵鬧鬧的幣圈與區塊鏈世界，協議們總是搶著提出更高的利率以打贏搶攻市佔率的戰爭，但卻忽略使用者的風險。伊莉莎白鄧教授 2014 年出版的《Happy Money》列舉出多項金錢與快樂之間的關係（研究在幾年後有更新），追逐財富的你可能也很適合閱讀。「永不愚蠢」更多是參考了對中國（或全世界）高度競爭社會裡年輕人心裡的焦慮，也同時討論資訊監控的可能問題。「永不無聊」則意指 Netflix、Disney+ 等提供的無限娛樂，反思我們花了大把時間與劇中及劇外人建立的關係。最後以「永不是你」作結，講起飛後重摔，多半又會再被捧飛的元宇宙裡，雖然承諾了全新的美好世界與生活，但承諾時卻故意遺漏了資源仍然稀缺，競爭仍然存在的事實。

　　我雖然對這些故事多少有些詮釋，但我不想講太多霸佔讀者解釋故事的方式，也不想僵化你的想像空間，我們還是獨立思考後多交流想法，才能一起前進。

　　小狐狸的角色設定時也經過了許多思考，最終的透明設定是為了凸顯創業家們或是科技從業者希望被看到被認可，甚至找到存在意義的初衷。同時也提醒存在意義大概不會在財富或成功的累積中找到，而會從人們的相對關係出現。如果資本額或營收數字不是你每年的 KPI，你會怎麼設定營運目標？1917 年道奇兄弟控訴有名的亨利福特一案中，密西根州高等法院給了明確的回答：「一個商業公司設立和運行的主要目的是為股東創造利潤。」我很同意，但是一百年後我們有了其他選擇，GDP 不再是衡量國家經濟的唯一標準，2008 不丹政府開始嘗試 Gross National Happiness 國民快樂指數，每年新聞都會報導全球各國快樂指數的排名（台灣的排名並不如想像的那麼落後）。區塊鏈協議開始嘗試去中心化的社會架構與治理方式，許多跟社會公共財相關的議題都有新的實驗方向。如果國家都開始嘗試新的衡量指標，那組織或個人也許也可以。

1987 年奧斯卡・阿里亞斯・桑切斯因為對中美洲的和平做出貢獻而得到諾貝爾和平獎，他曾說過「我喜歡造橋，而不是築牆。」我在帕森設計學院的研究中寫過同樣的話，也為此設計了遊戲解決五十多人的組織裡小社交圈彼此排斥所帶來的問題。我所設計的遊戲自然沒有辦法跟諾貝爾和平獎做比較，但我看到的是當人願意開始彼此了解傾聽與對話，而不是在對話前預設立場或貼上標籤，很多事都能應運而解。小狐狸在最終章因看到橋上互相對話的人們而了解到了自我價值與存在意義，這些橋促進了彼此幫助、互通有無，也讓某些角色追逐夢想、走得更遠。

No Place Is Utopia。《迷航烏托邦》希望傳達的訊息是科技不是萬靈丹，科技跟技術本身沒有對錯，但科技追求絕對不能是唯一追求。無論科技有多大的躍進，不過就是把同樣的一群人從光譜的一端推到另外一端，光譜底層的仍然是同一群人，人性仍然破碎缺陷，我們還是需要解決人的問題。我父親以前跟我說過做人比做事更重要，二十出頭的我哪裡聽得懂，只覺得把事做好就結了，懶得跟人政治來心機去，現在才知道做人的確比做事更重要，如果人的問題解決了，事情大概也成了一半。烏托邦在希臘文裡的真正意思，就是 No place，在歷史上所有討論烏托邦哲學的文獻裡，都講過烏托邦只是個追逐的目標，但我們從來沒有想要真正到達目的地。「Utopia is no place, and it's ok.」。

巫女在請小狐狸選擇槌子時總是重複著重量的一致性。重量是小狐狸的能力，大小則是小狐狸的野心，他們的相對關係是我對快樂的理解。當野心大於能力太多時，失敗的機率高，就像碎裂的大槌子一樣，失去的多半要比獲得的更多。當野心小於能力太多時，成就的機會小，就像那座迷你橋一樣，讓人毫無成就感。當野心等同於能力時，人不過就是在原地踏步，木橋雖然扎實有用，但卻毫無挑戰。人生或職場的快樂取決於設定期望的智慧，將野心設定的比能力稍微大一點，人生才能前進，才有探索，才有成長。

　　其他當然還是多少有一些小隱喻，譬如說爲什麼大部分角色都是男性呢？看看現在科技業的男女比例應該不難想像原因。

　　我曾經寫過一篇文章〈你的新創並沒有讓世界更好〉，我們因應客戶的「需求」並從中賺取利潤，但我們很少思考需求被滿足後對個人或是社會造成的影響。根據 World Drug Report 2017 到 2020 年暗網上的毒品販賣量體相較於 2010 到 2017 年間成長了四倍，這是個極端需求被滿足，但對整體社會或個人都沒有幫助的例子。虛擬貨幣可能也是好例子，2022 Terra 區塊鏈的崩盤造成不知多少自殺案例。這並不是說科技不該進步，或是不該累積個人財富，而是在我們了解這個世界怎麼運作、人類怎麼行爲後，世界上的科技組織不但要存活，還應該運用這些知識將世界導向正軌。賺錢不難，但做好事賺錢才是我們應該承接的任務。這是我給科技產業的挑戰，也是我給自己的挑戰。

　　造橋，別築牆。

迷航烏托邦:科技世界讓人生迷路,但你依舊還可以很幸福 /Noah 作 .-- 一版 .-- 臺北市:時報文化出版企業股份有限公司, 2023.01

面；　　公分 .-- (大人國 ; 9)

ISBN 978-626-353-268-7(精裝)

1.CST: 生活態度 2.CST: 修身

192.1　　　　　　　　　　　　　　　　　　　　　　　　　111020299

ISBN 978-626-353-268-7
Printed in Taiwan

大人國 009

迷航烏托邦：科技世界讓人生迷路，但你依舊還可以很幸福

作者　葉向林 Noah ｜ 繪圖　披薩先生 ｜ 主編　謝翠鈺 ｜ 企劃　鄭家謙 ｜ 封面設計　披薩先生 ｜ 美術編輯　SHRTING WU ｜ 董事長　趙政岷 ｜ 出版者　時報文化出版企業股份有限公司　108019 台北市和平西路三段 240 號 7 樓　發行專線―(02)2306-6842　讀者服務專線―0800-231-705・(02)2304-7103　讀者服務傳真―(02)2304-6858　郵撥―19344724 時報文化出版公司　信箱―10899 台北華江橋郵局第九九信箱　時報悅讀網― http://www.readingtimes.com.tw　法律顧問　理律法律事務所　陳長文律師、李念祖律師 ｜ 印刷　文聯印刷有限公司 ｜ 一版一刷　2023 年 1 月 18 日 ｜ 定價　新台幣 480 元 ｜ 缺頁或破損的書，請寄回更換